How Much Is $1.oo?

Carey Molter

Consulting Editor, Monica Marx, M.A./Reading Specialist

ABDO
Publishing Company

Published by SandCastle™, an imprint of ABDO Publishing Company, 4940 Viking Drive, Edina, Minnesota 55435.

Credits
Edited by: Pam Price
Curriculum Coordinator: Nancy Tuminelly
Cover and Interior Design and Production: Mighty Media
Photo Credits: Hemera Studio, PhotoDisc, Stockbyte

Library of Congress Cataloging-in-Publication Data

Molter, Carey, 1973-
    How much is $1.00? / Carey Molter.
      p. cm. -- (Dollars & cents)
    Includes index.
    Summary: Explains what a one dollar bill is, how it compares to other dollar bills, and how many singles are needed to purchase different items.
    ISBN 1-57765-892-2
    1. Money--Juvenile literature. 2. Dollar, American--Juvenile literature. [1. Money.] I.
Title: How much is one dollar?. II. Title. III. Series.

    HG221.5 .M6534 2002   2002071709
    332.4'973--dc21

SandCastle™ books are created by a professional team of educators, reading specialists, and content developers around five essential components that include phonemic awareness, phonics, vocabulary, text comprehension, and fluency. All books are written, reviewed, and leveled for guided reading, early intervention reading, and Accelerated Reader® programs and designed for use in shared, guided, and independent reading and writing activities to support a balanced approach to literacy instruction.

Let Us Know

After reading the book, SandCastle would like you to tell us your stories about reading. What is your favorite page? Was there something hard that you needed help with? Share the ups and downs of learning to read. We want to hear from you! To get posted on the ABDO Publishing Company Web site, send us email at:

sandcastle@abdopub.com

SandCastle Level: Beginning

How much is one dollar?

This is a one-dollar bill.

One dollar is the same as one hundred pennies.

This is how to write one dollar.

$1.00

One dollar is the same as twenty nickels.

 =

One dollar is the same as
ten dimes.

One dollar is the same as four quarters.

This hat costs $1.00.

That is one dollar.

This deck of cards
cost $2.00.

That is two dollars.

$3.00

This toy costs $3.00.

That is three dollars.

$4.00

How many dollars does this toy cost?

(four)

Picture Index

cards, p. 17

one-dollar bill, p. 5

hat, p. 15

one dollar,
pp. 3, 7, 9, 11, 13, 15

More about the One-Dollar Bill

President George Washington

All bills have the signature of the secretary of the treasury

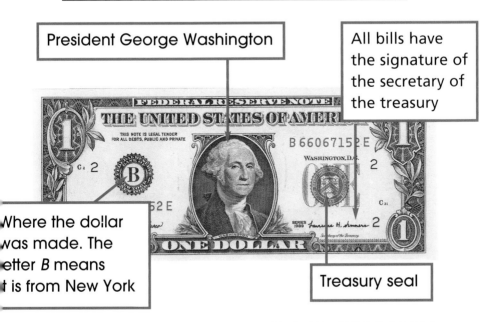

Where the dollar was made. The letter *B* means it is from New York

Treasury seal

Presidential seal

About SandCastle™

A professional team of educators, reading specialists, and content developers created the SandCastle™ series to support young readers as they develop reading skills and strategies and increase their general knowledge. The SandCastle™ series has four levels that correspond to early literacy development in young children. The levels are provided to help teachers and parents select the appropriate books for young readers.

Emerging Readers
(no flags)

Beginning Readers
(1 flag)

Transitional Readers
(2 flags)

Fluent Readers
(3 flags)

These levels are meant only as a guide. All levels are subject to change.

To see a complete list of SandCastle™ books and other nonfiction titles from ABDO Publishing Company, visit www.abdopub.com or contact us at:

4940 Viking Drive, Edina, Minnesota 55435 • 1-800-800-1312 • fax: 1-952-831-1632